BONUS!

Pick up your FREE BONUS sweary word coloring pages!

Check out: **www.FckYeahColoring.com**

For more BONUS pages like this...

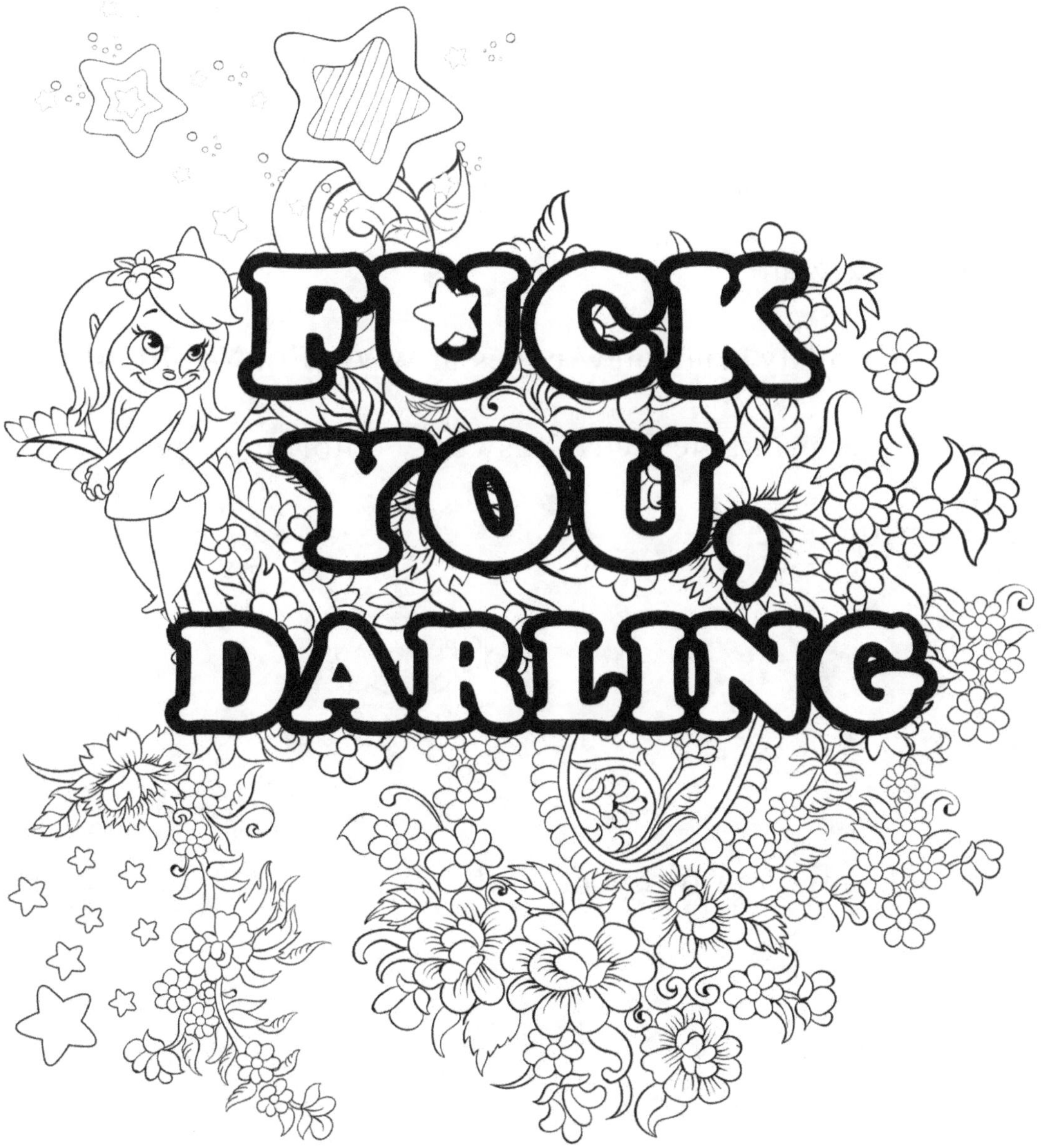

FUCK YOU, DARLING

Dear Creative,

Have a giggle and blow off some steam!

Look through the pages, and pick out the swears that speak to you at the moment.

Just remember, these pages are 18+ and not for the faint-hearted!

I send out NEW, FREE bonus pages every couple of weeks
as a special thank you.

Grab your ridiculously crude new pages at **www.FckYeahColoring.com**

Make sure you get printable BONUS sweary coloring pages

delivered immediately!

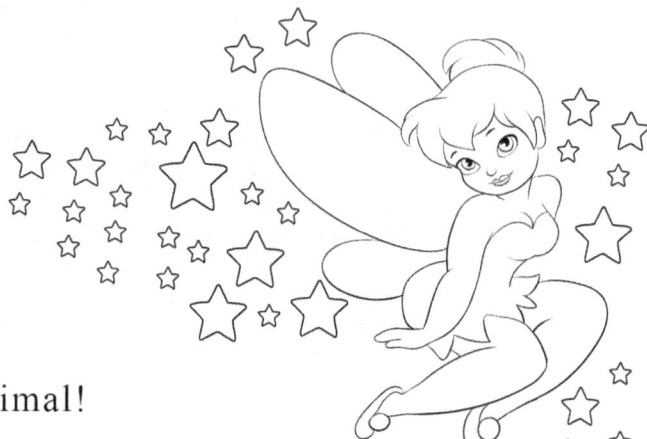

Now, enjoy coloring, you filthy animal!

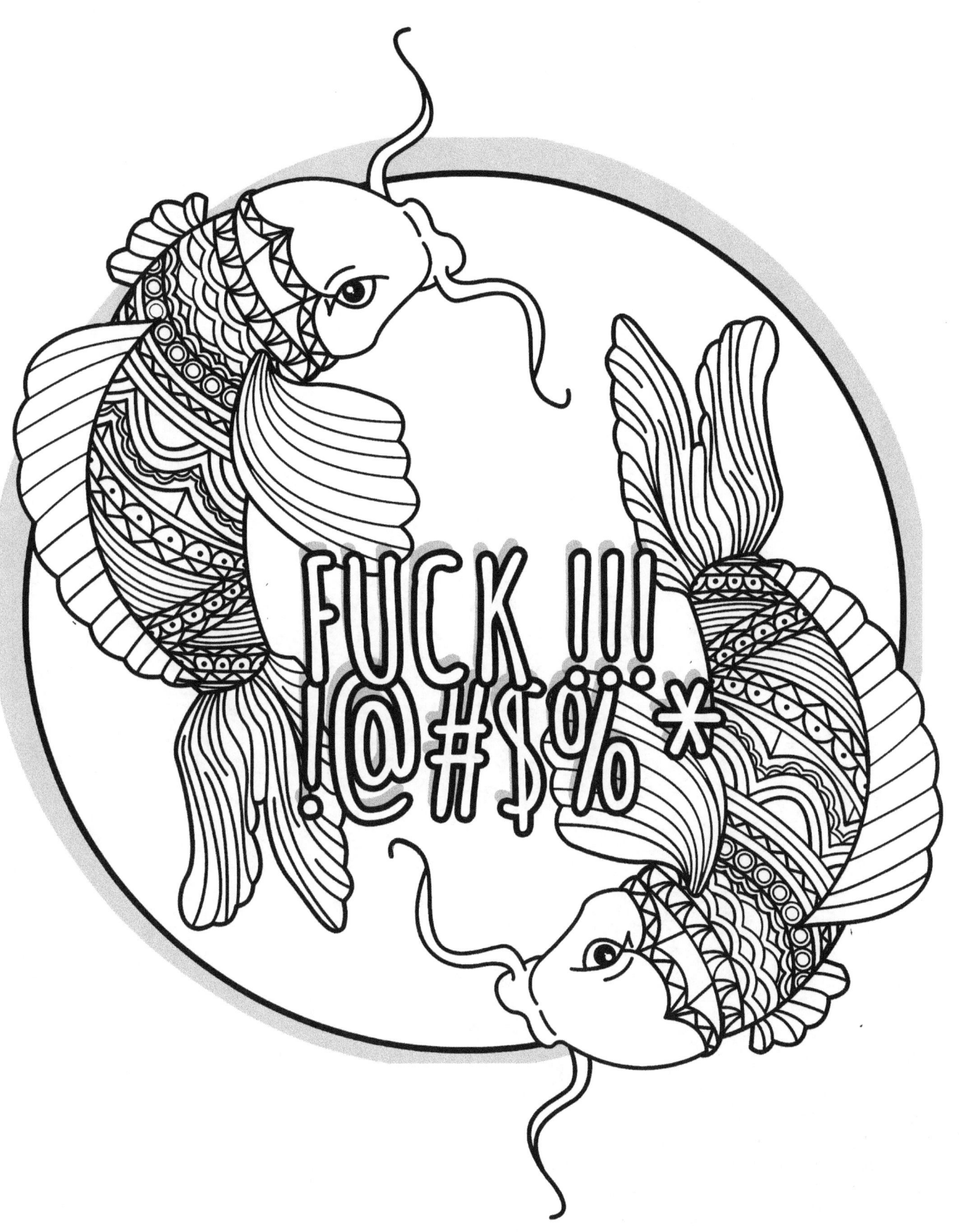

ISBN: 978-1523839667
By Artists:
    Mandala & Caricature Illustration
    Joshua Lazana Lagman and Jade Villaremo
Art Director: lluontheloose

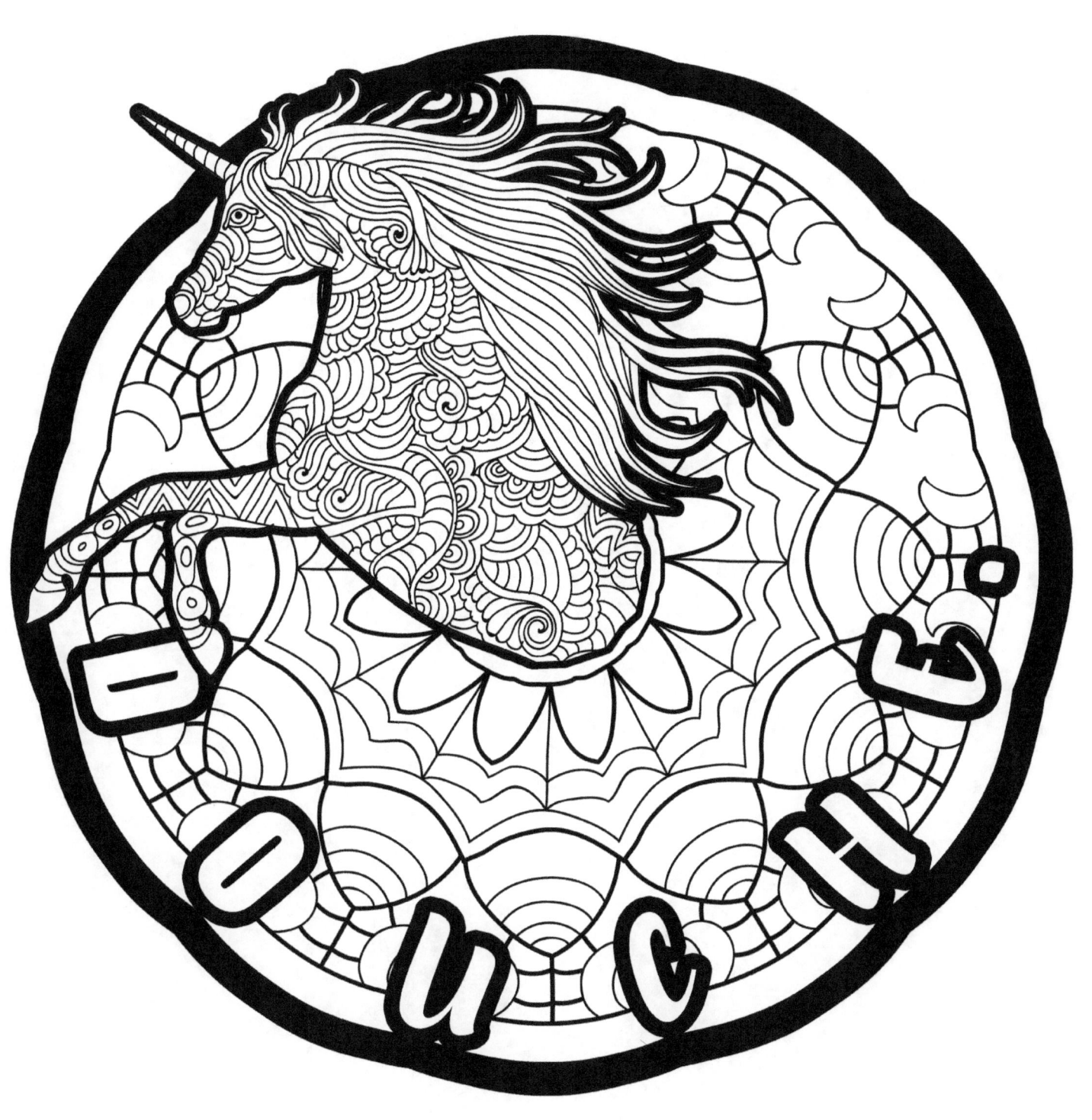

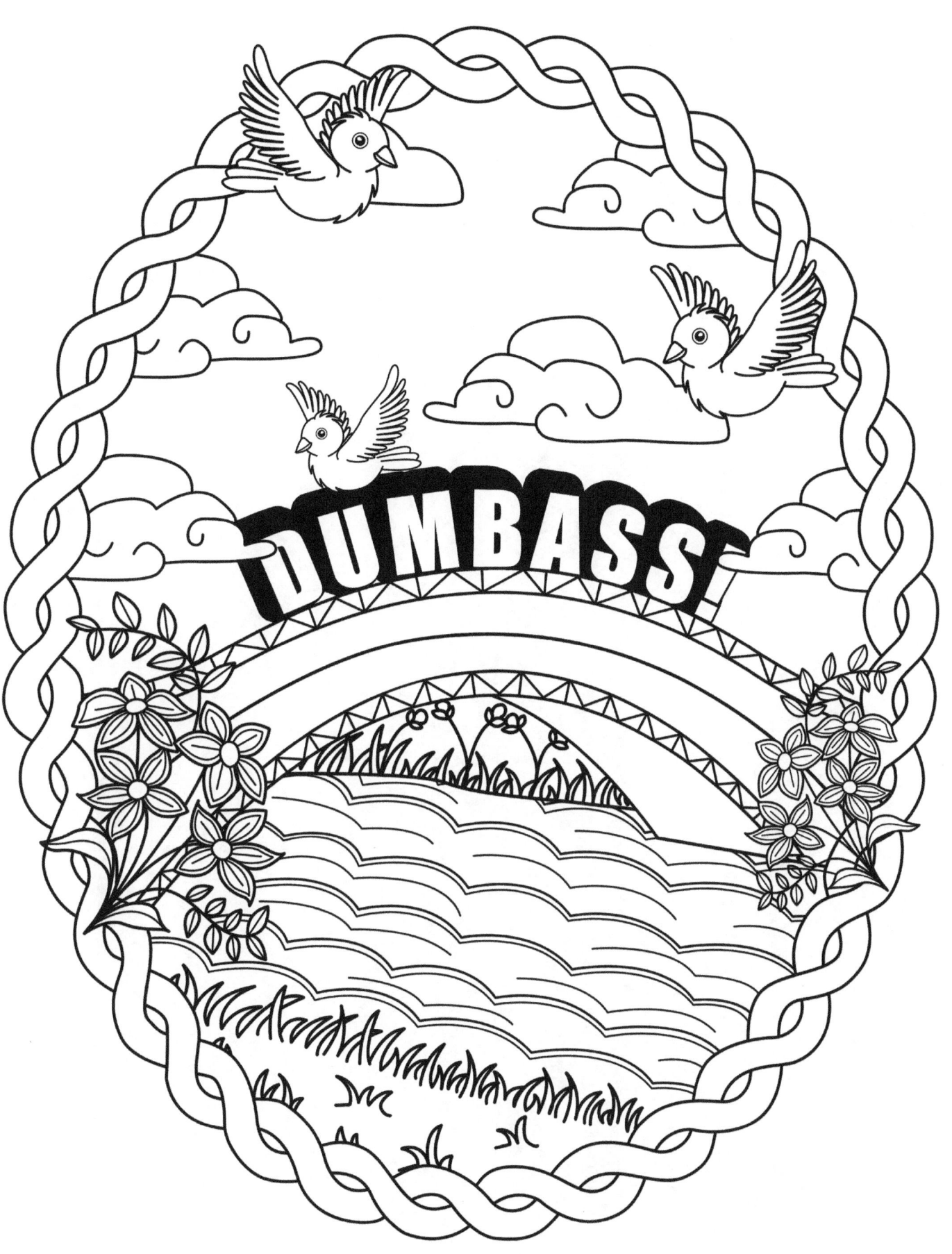

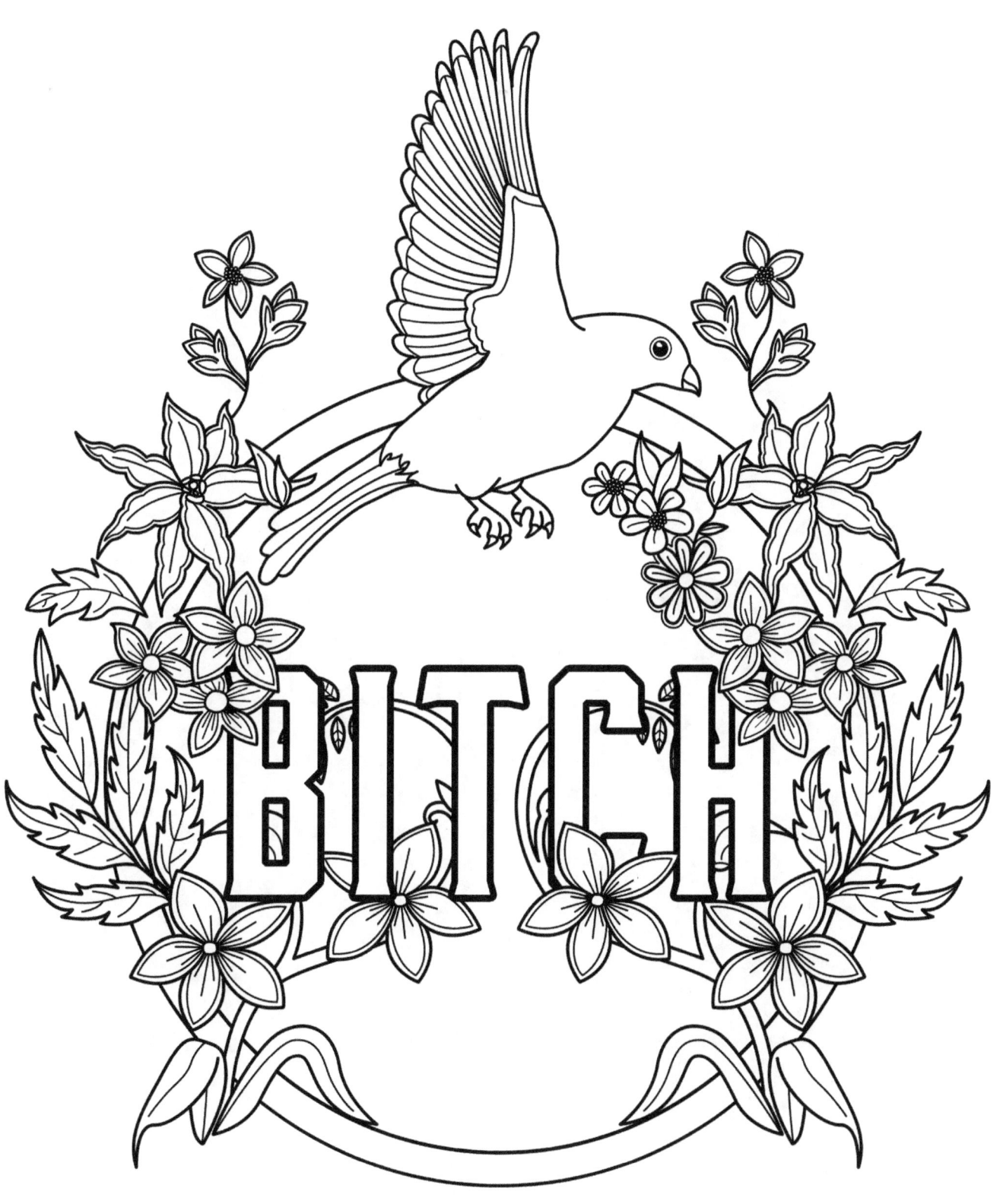

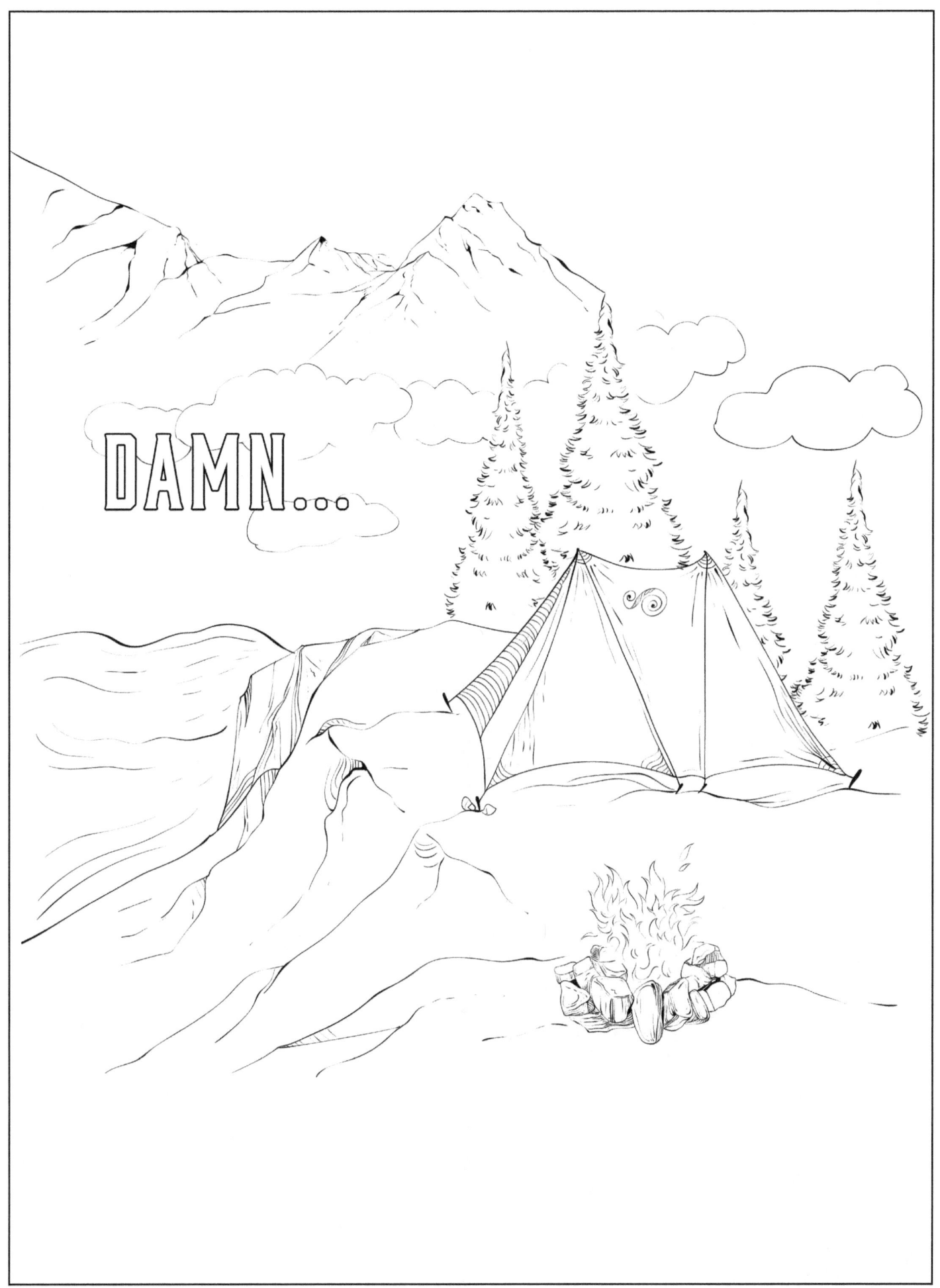

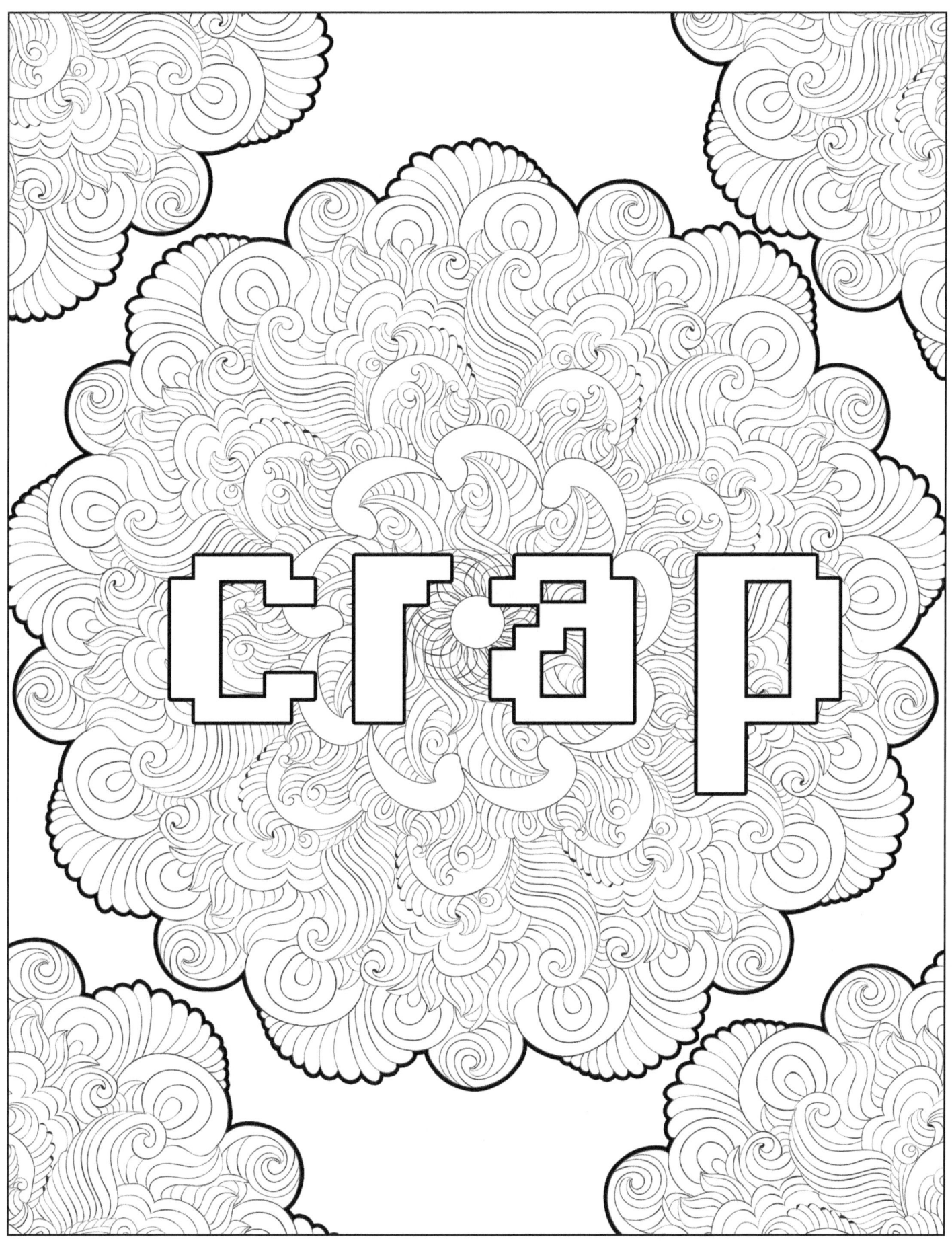

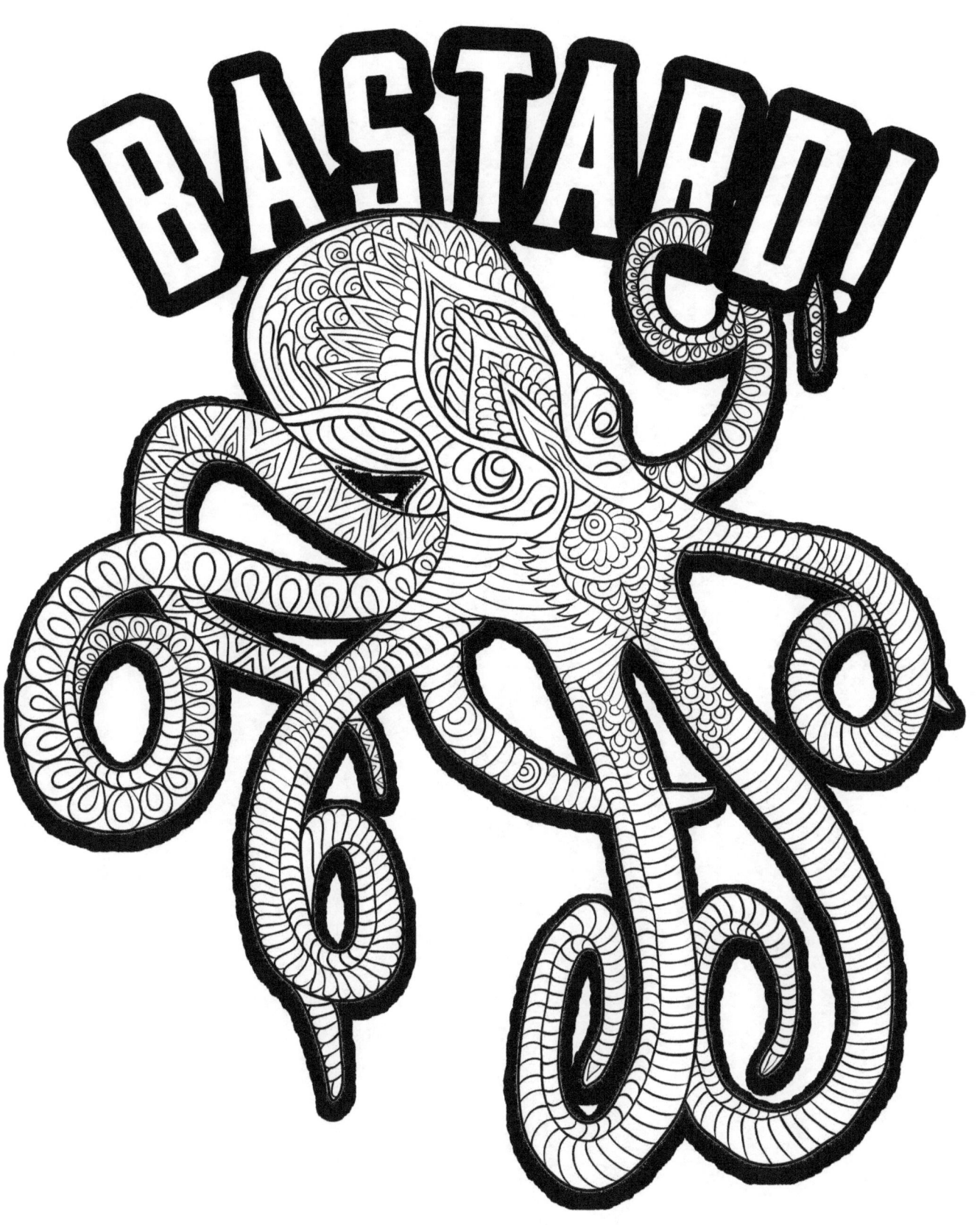

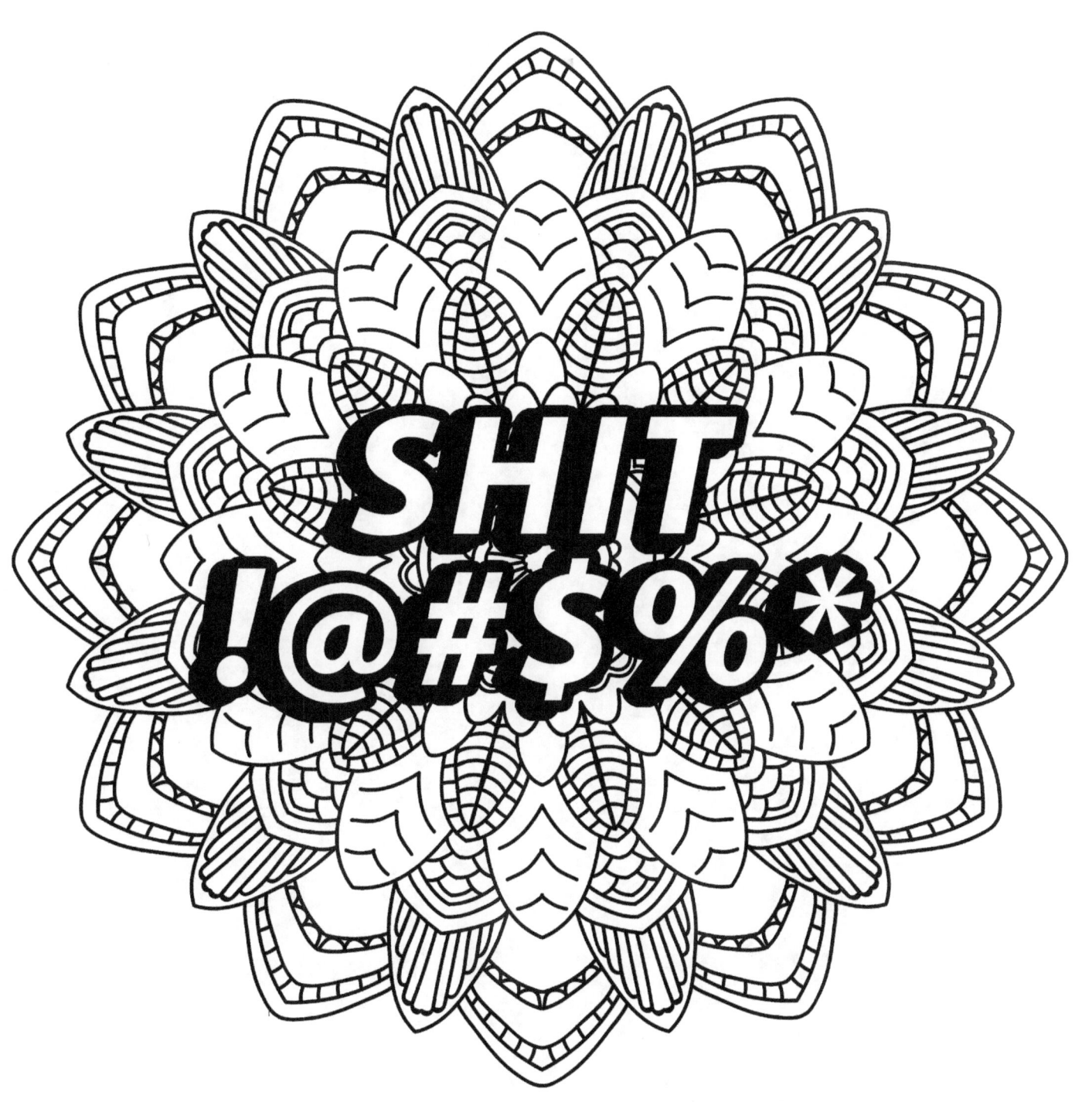

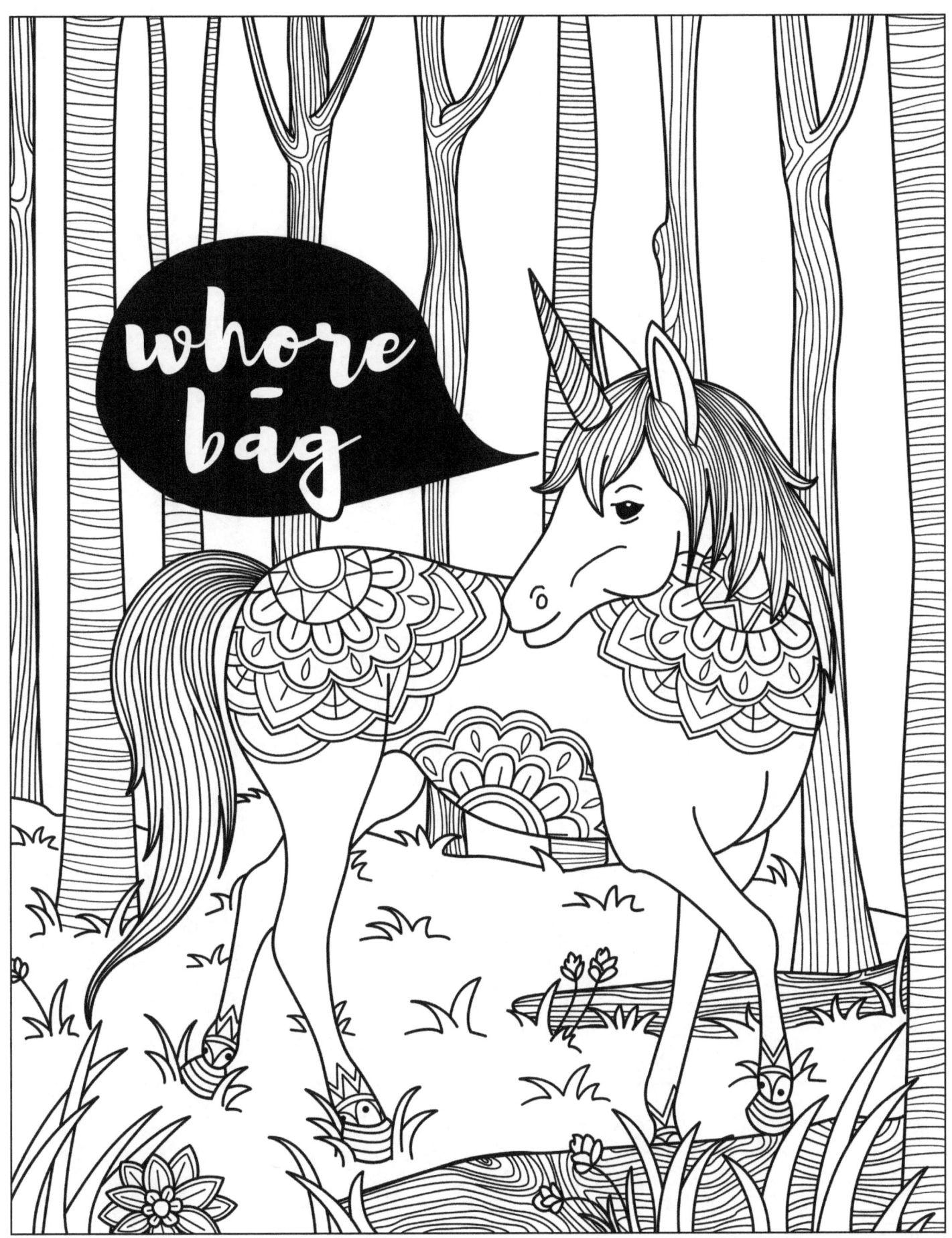

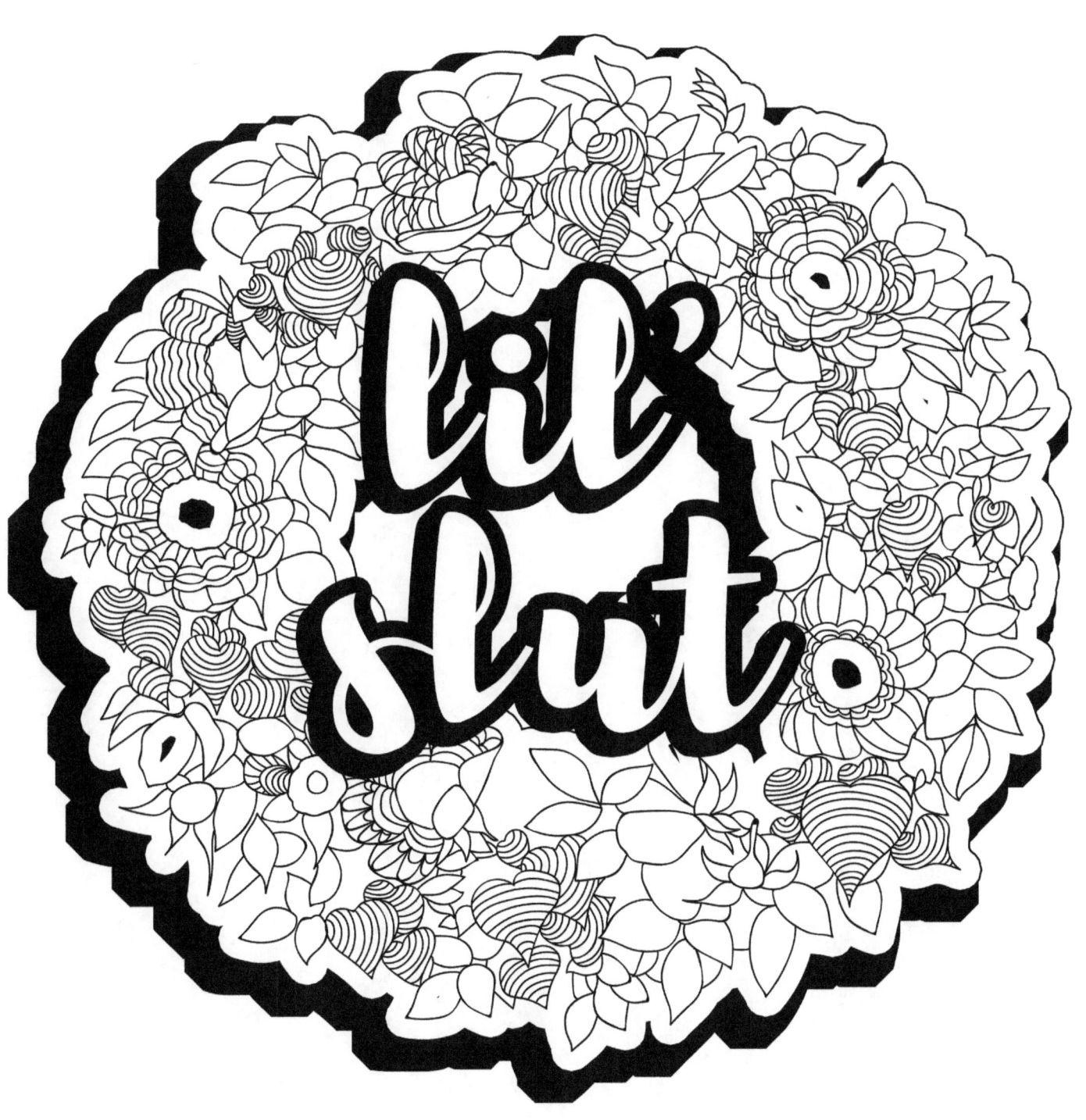

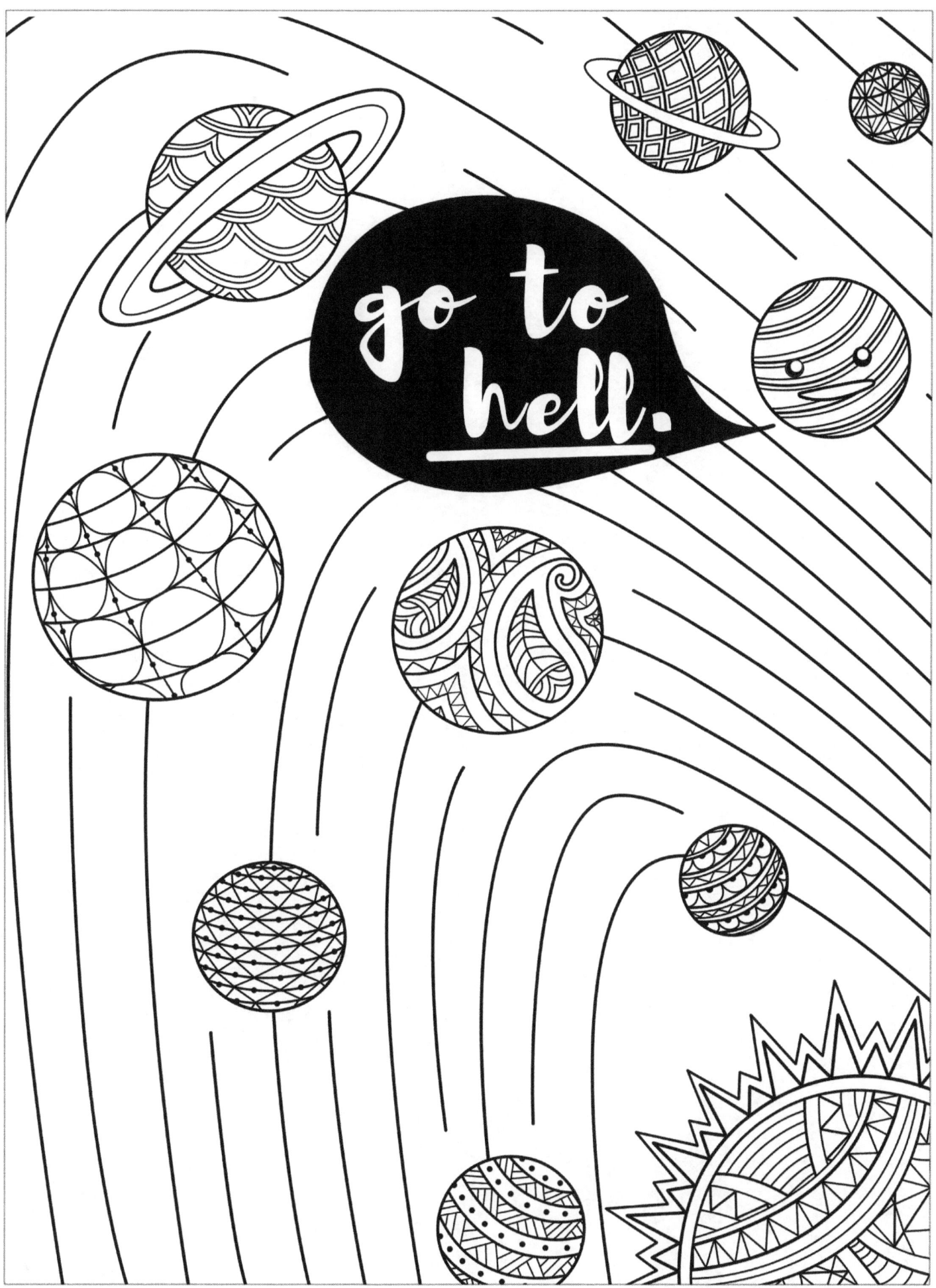

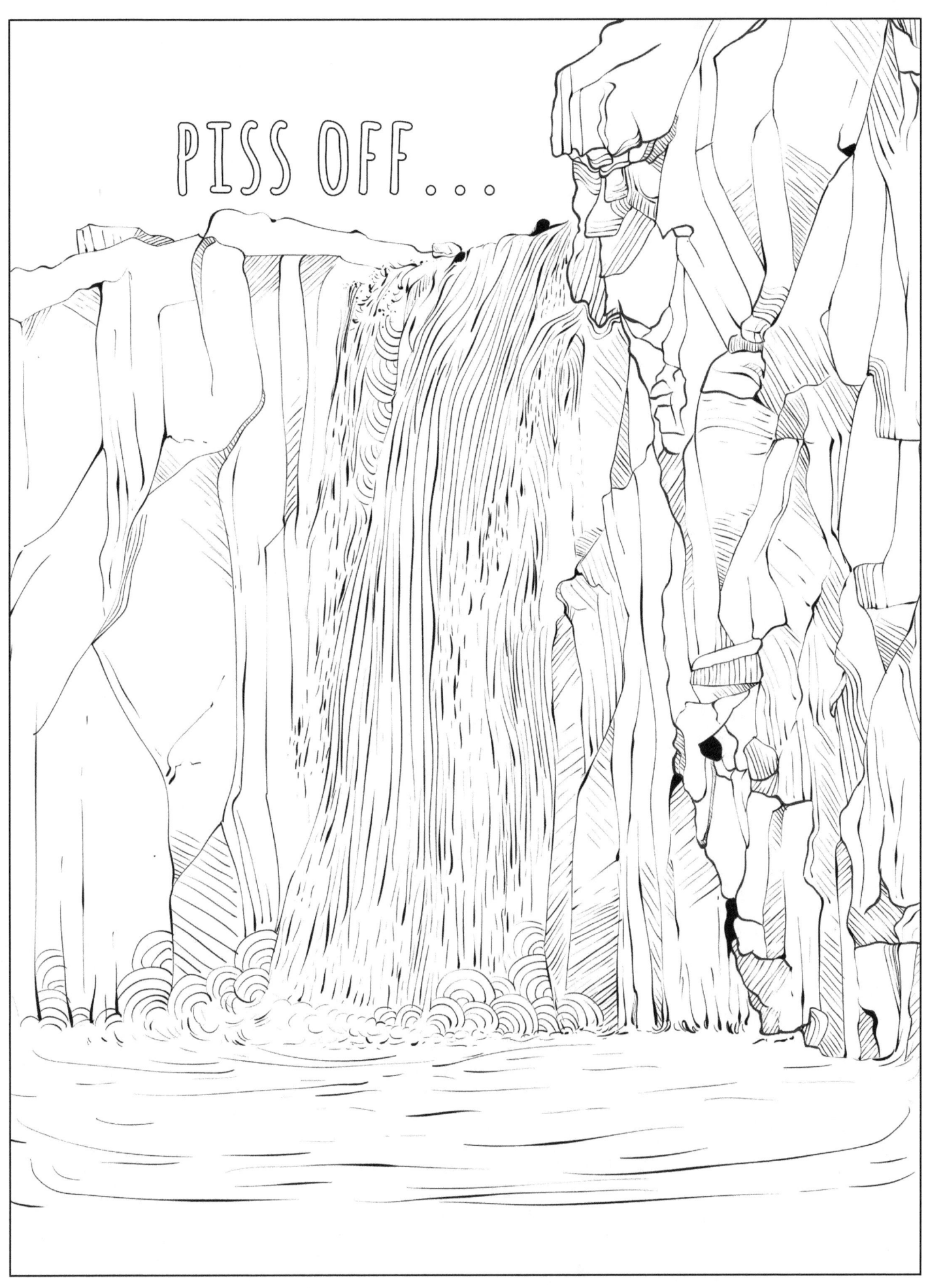

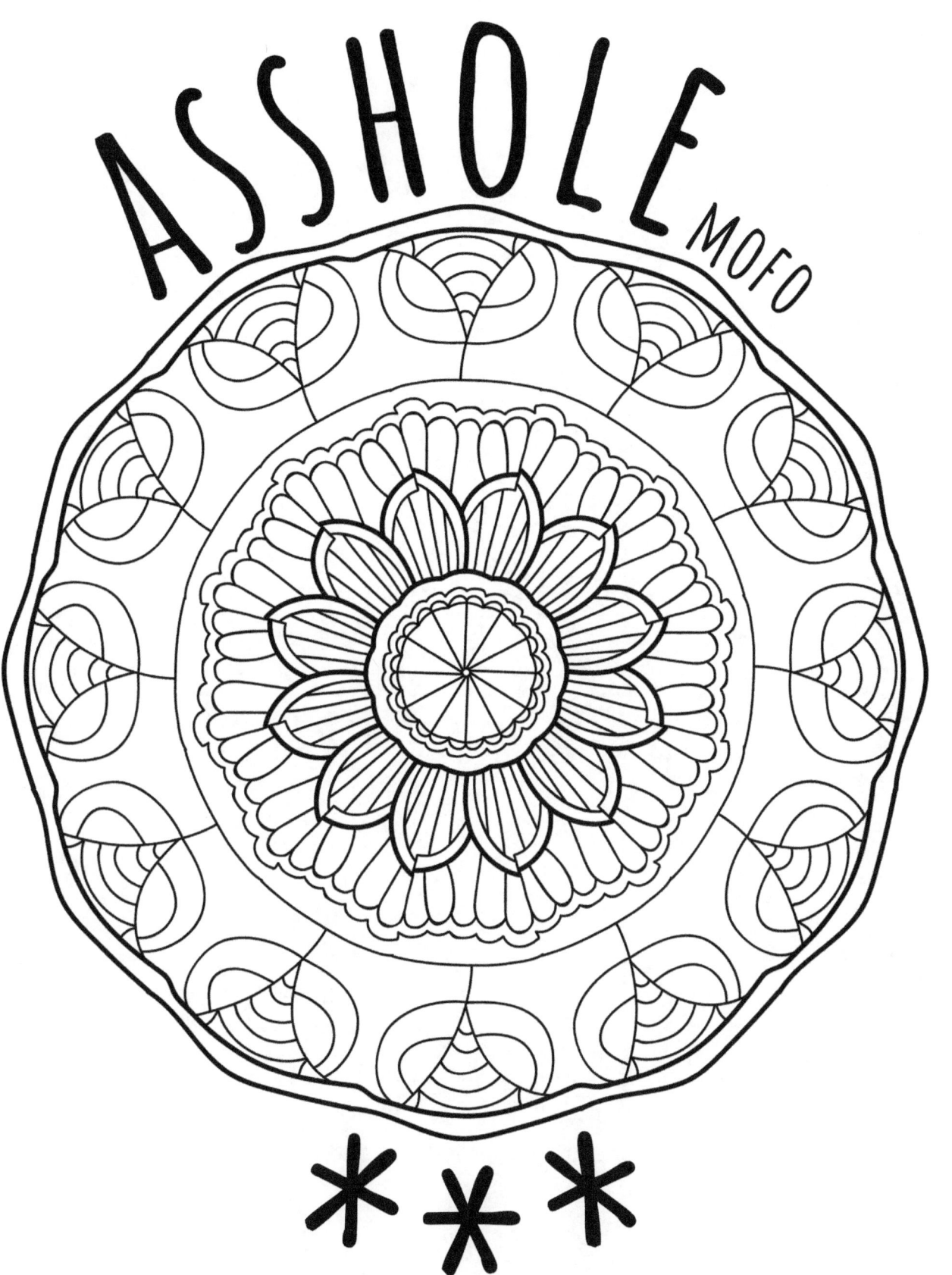

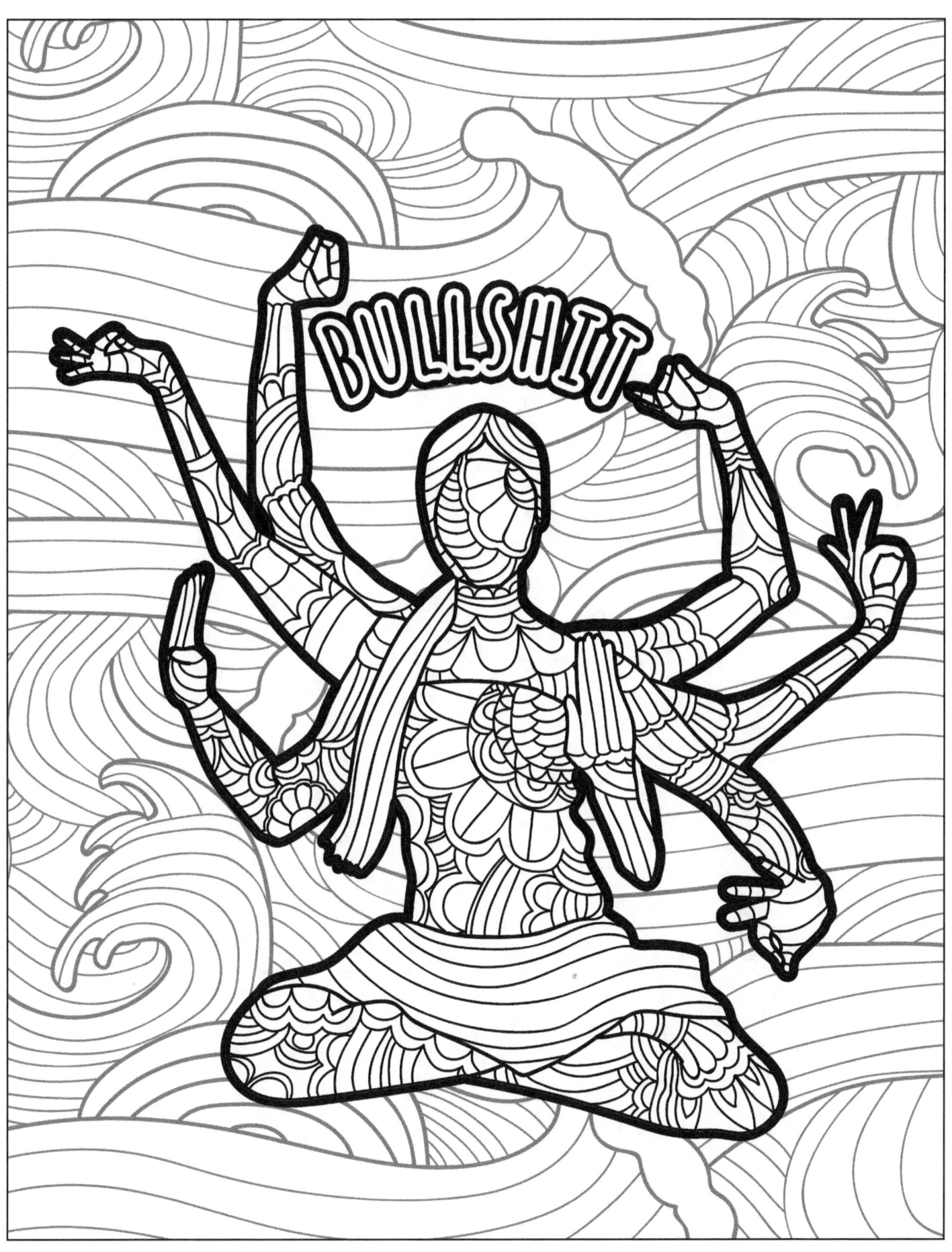

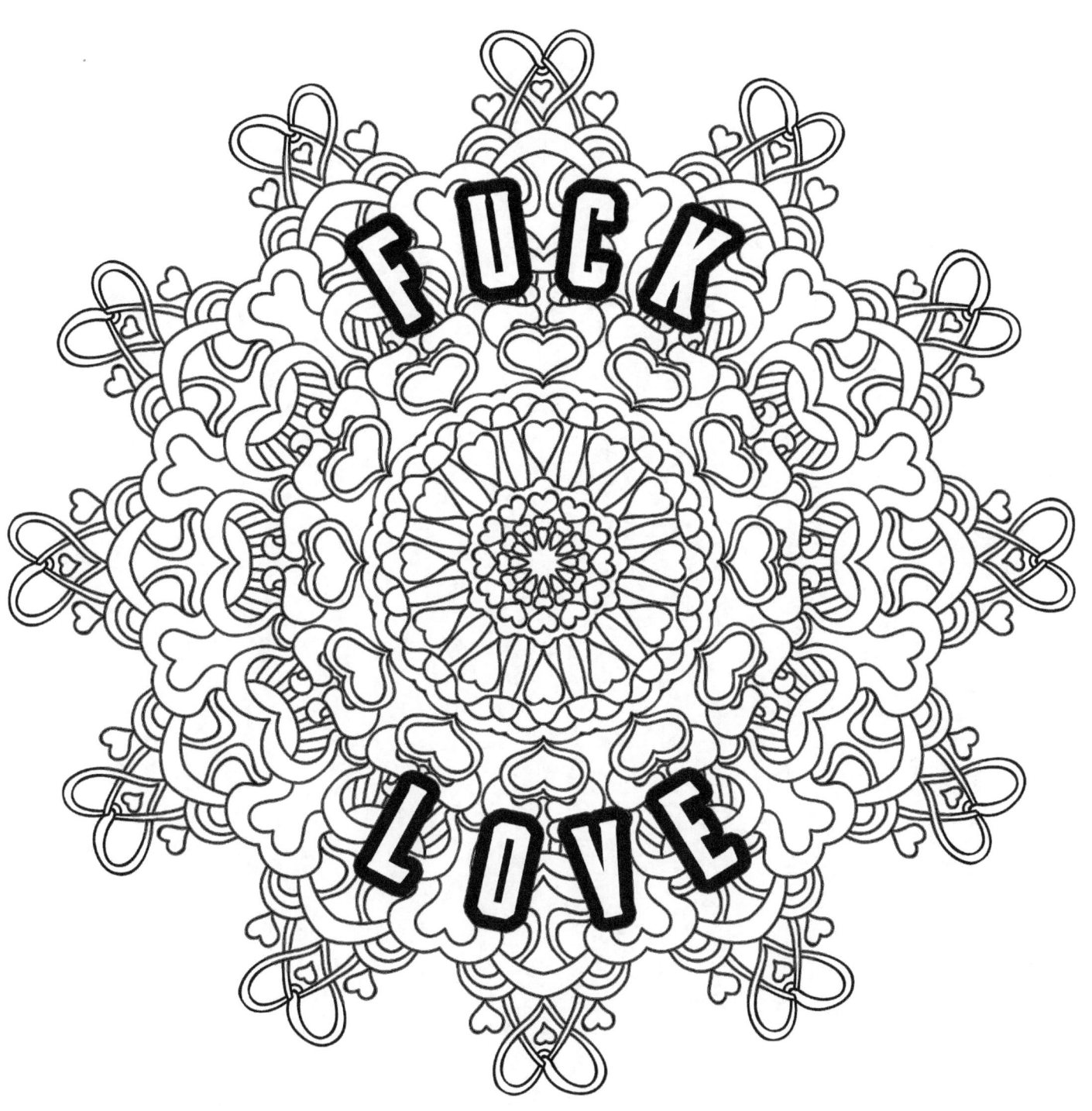

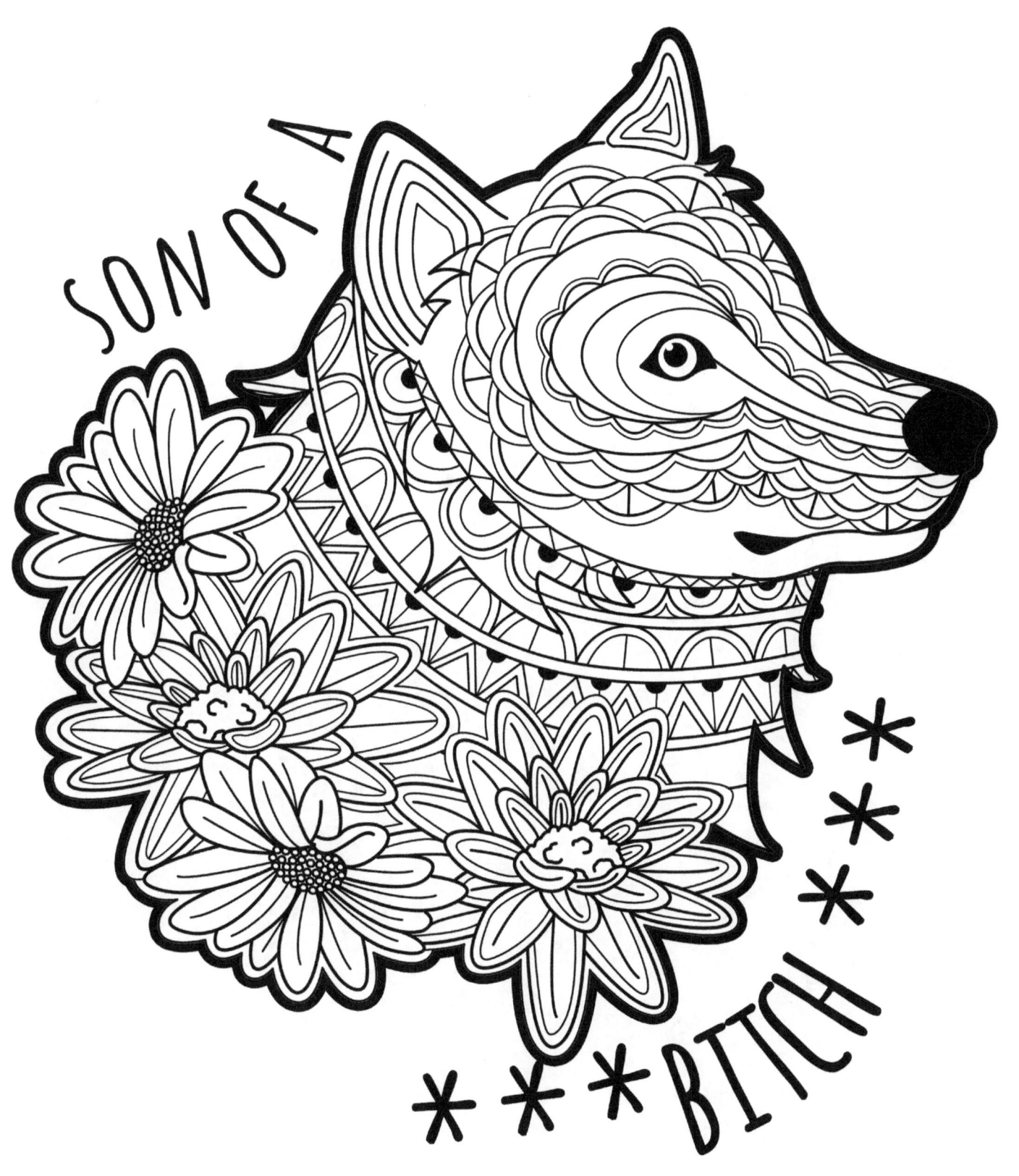

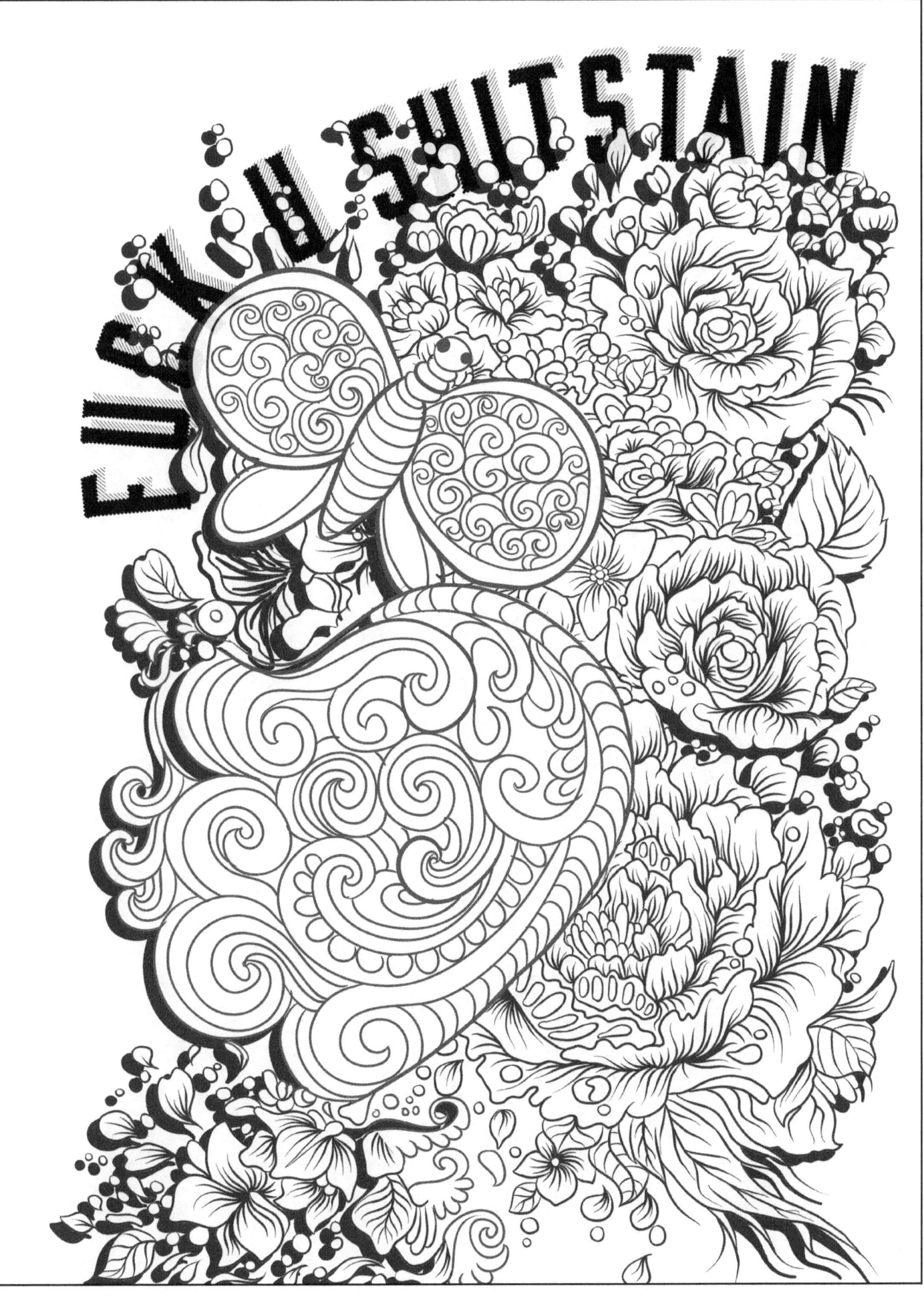

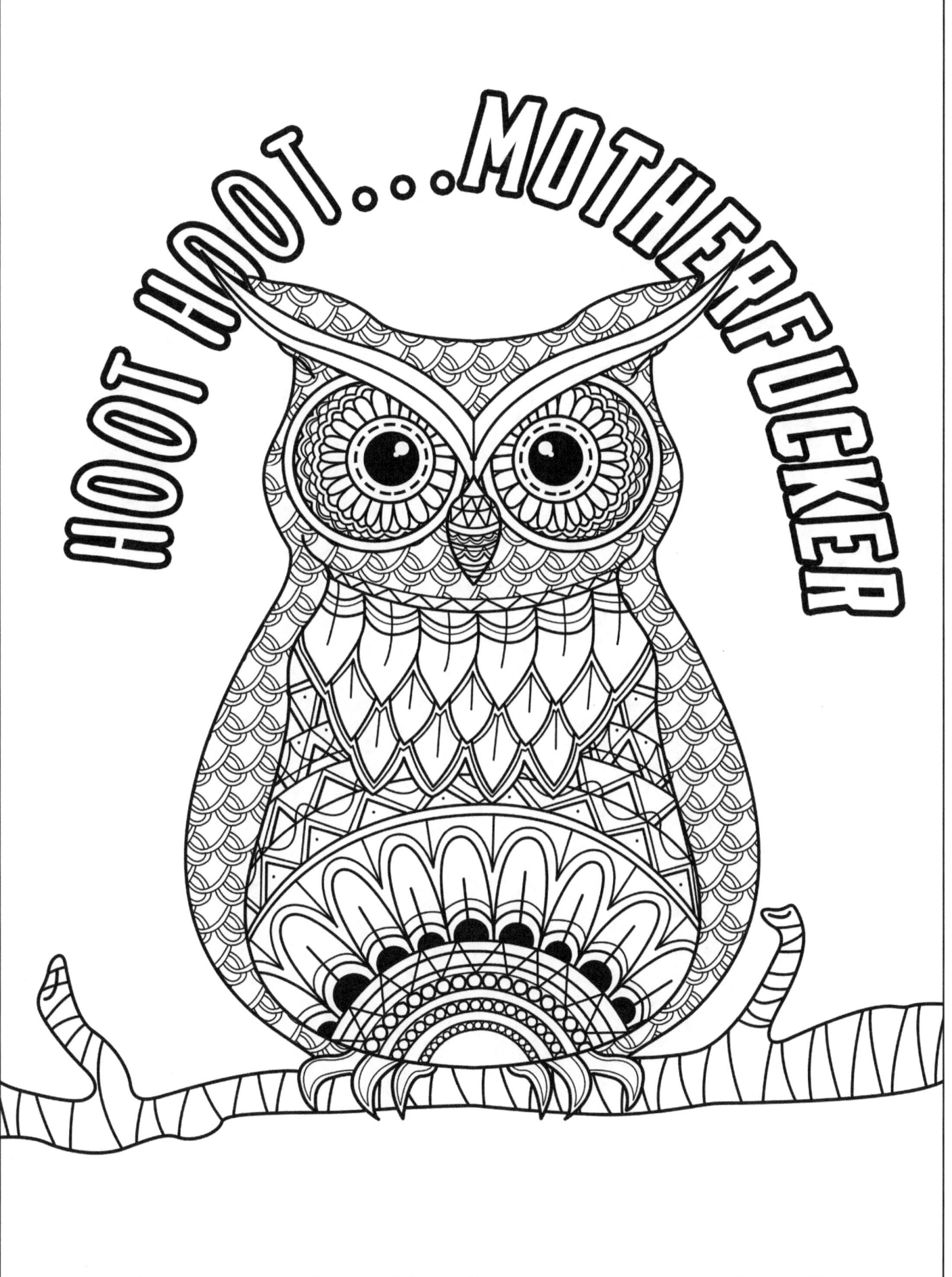

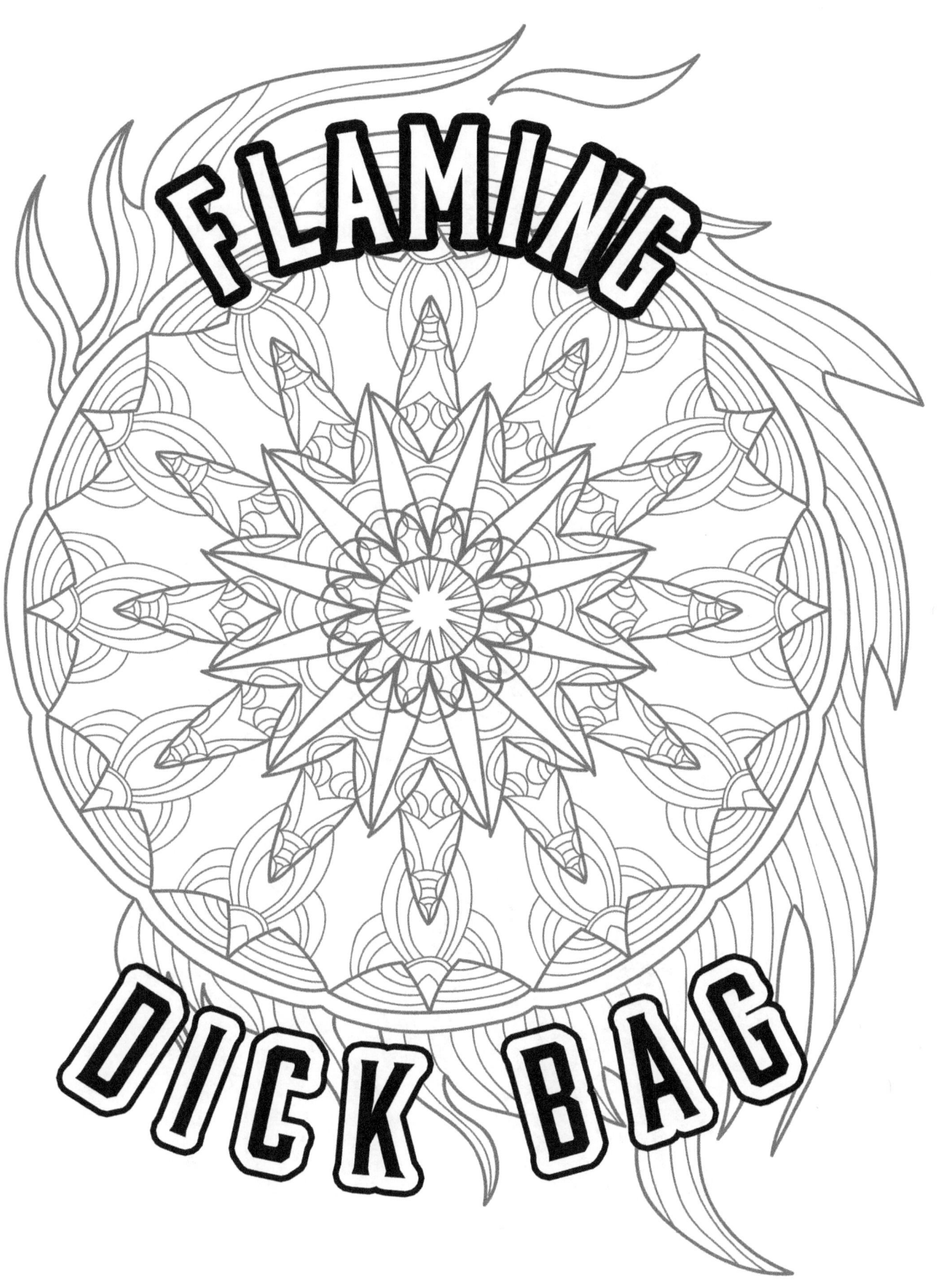

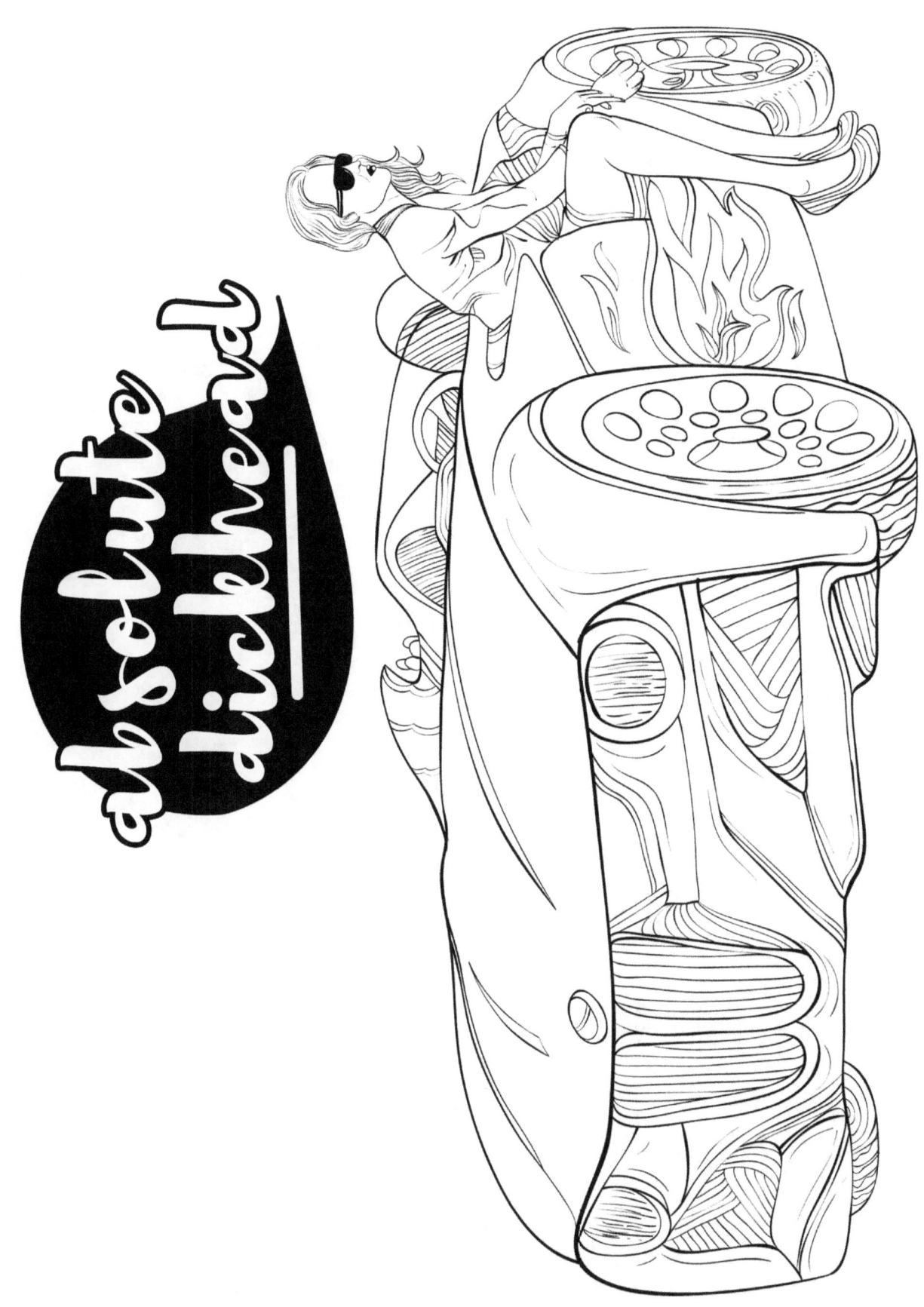

absolute
dickhead

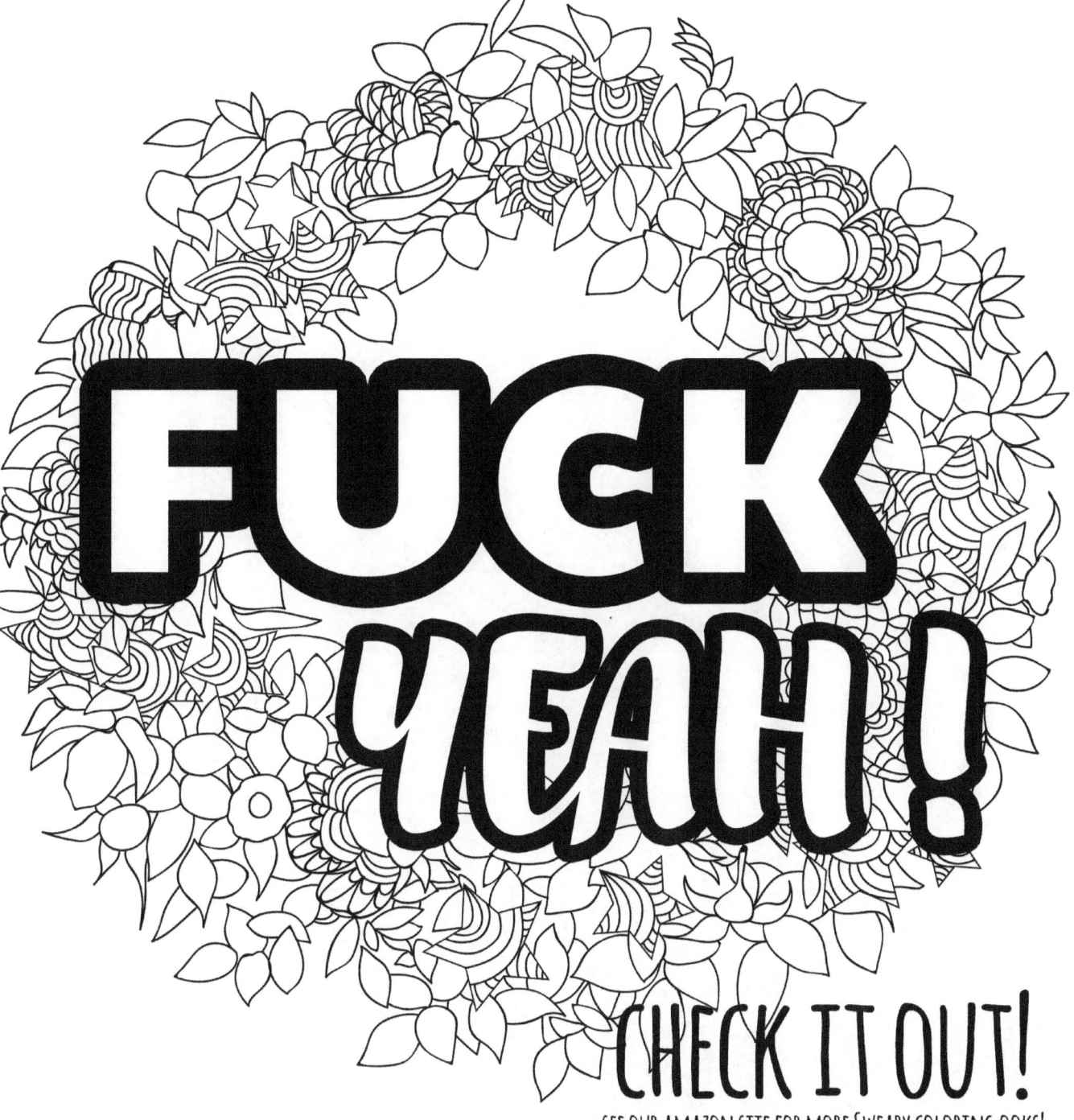

FUCK YEAH!

CHECK IT OUT!
SEE OUR AMAZON SITE FOR MORE Sweary coloring OOKS!

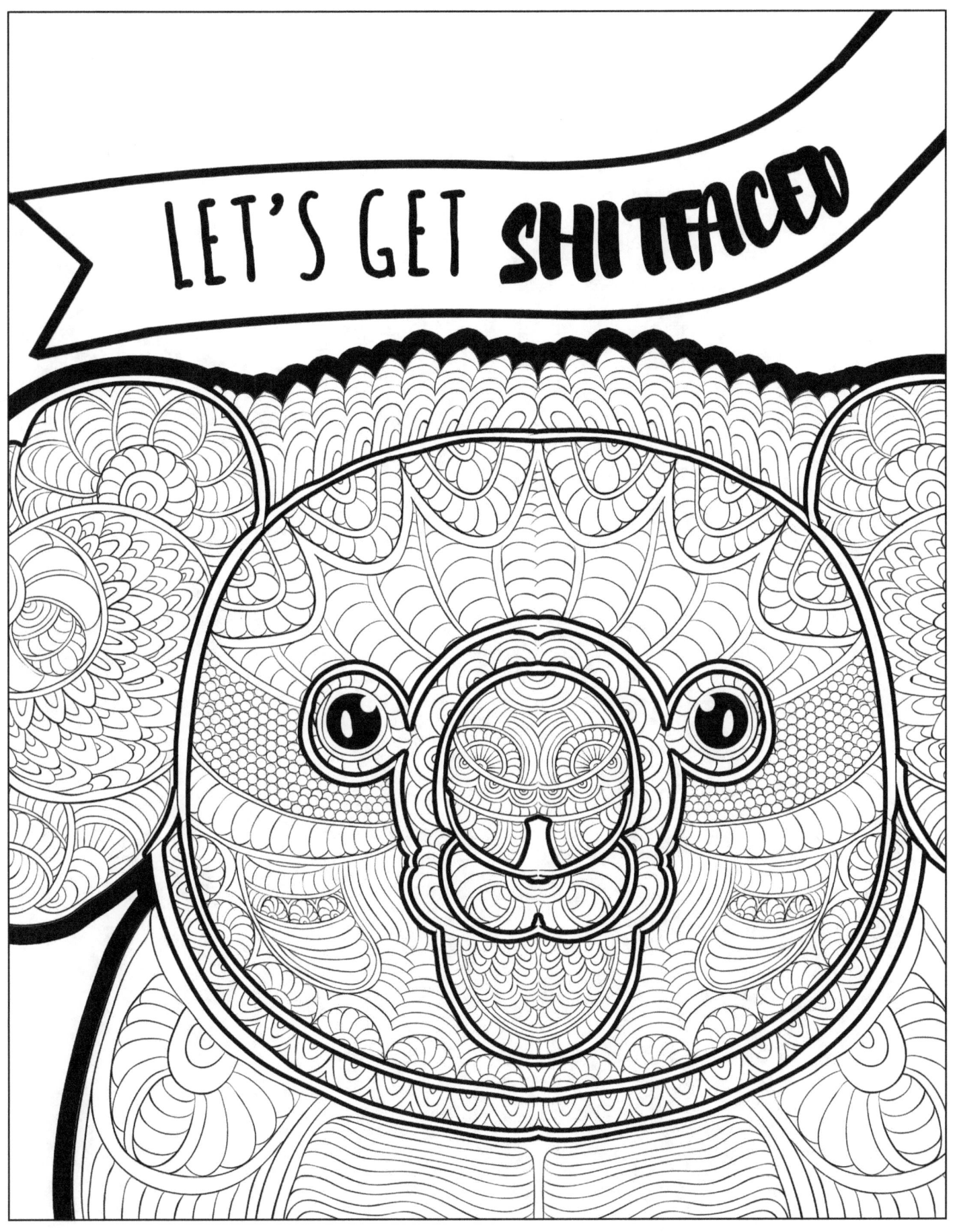

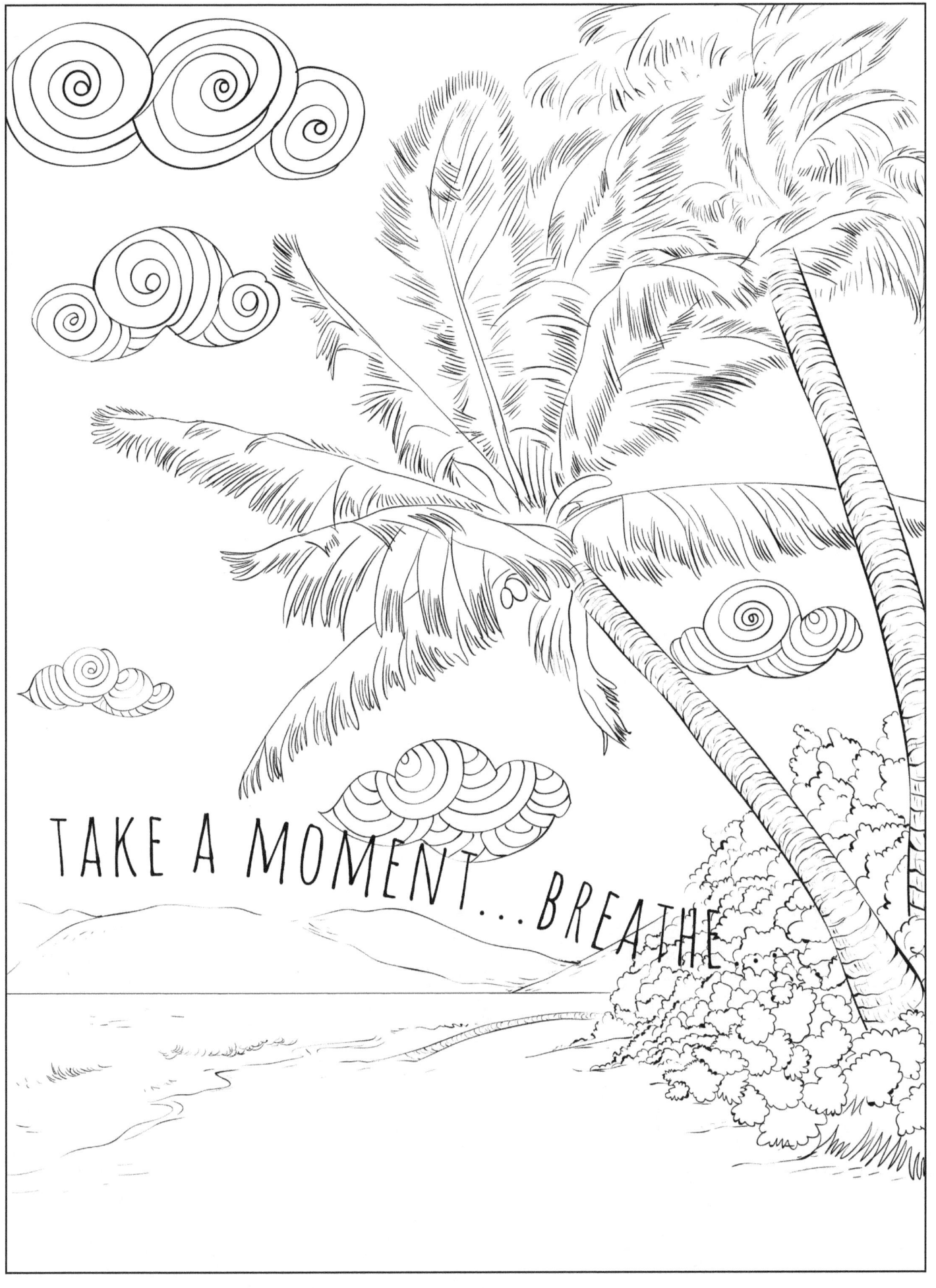

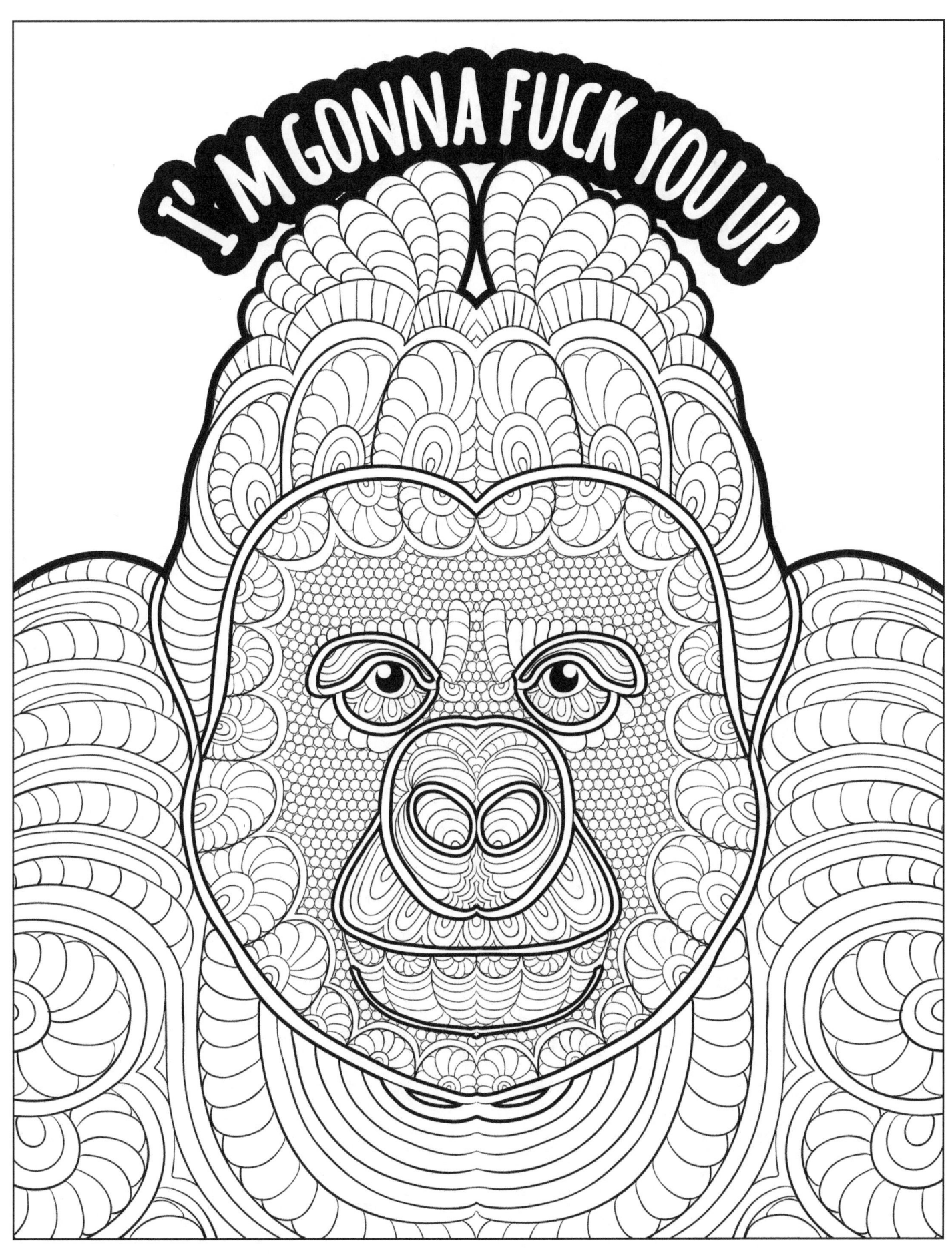

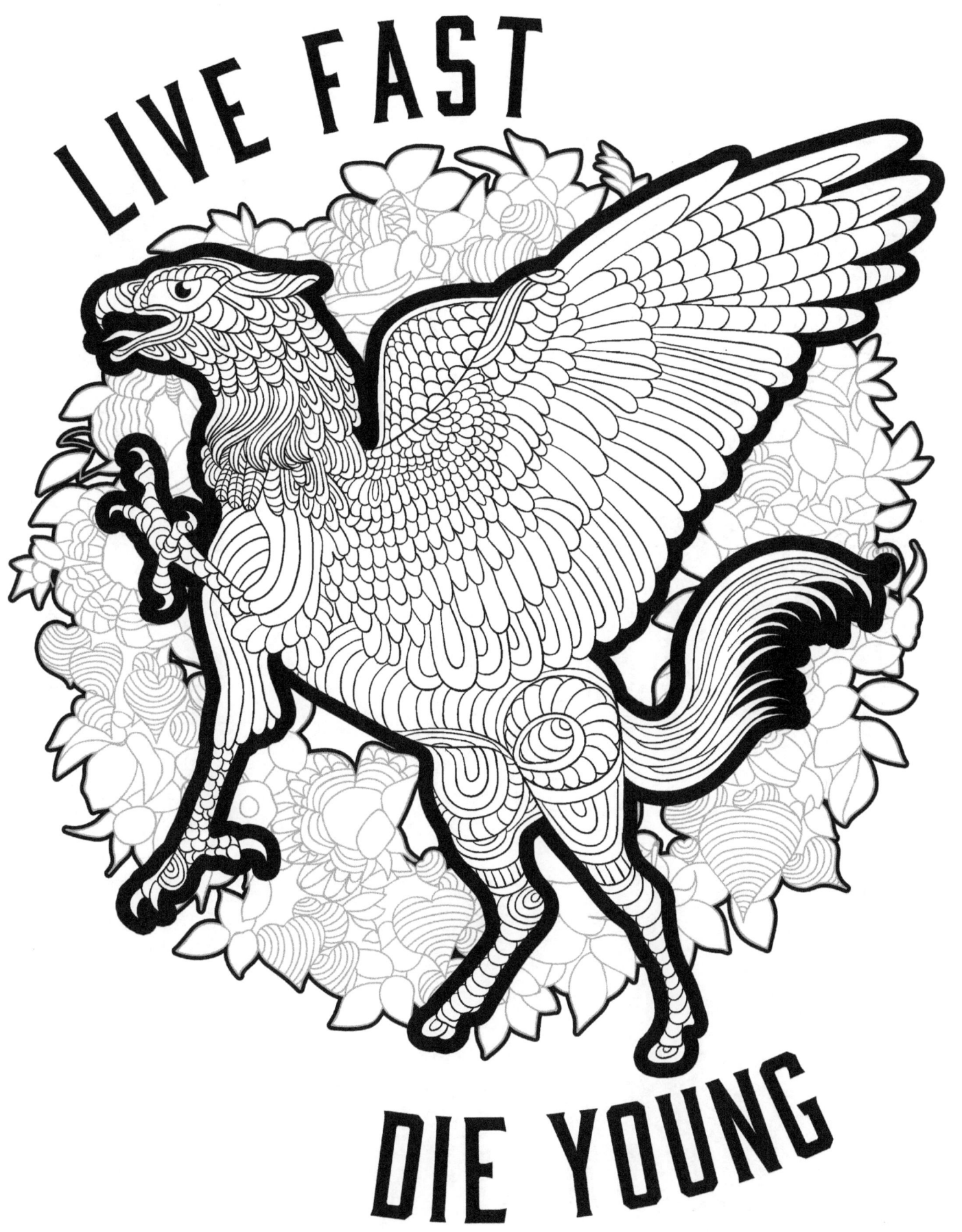